THANKS TO SAMI

SHE HELPED

THERE ONCE WAS A SCARECROW

STOOD IN A FIELD

ALONE

BIRDS FLEW BY

BUT WOULD NOT LAND NEAR

THE SCARECROW STOOD ALONE

THROUGH WIND

RAIN

AND SNOW

UNTIL ONE SUMMER

IN A DISTANT FIELD

A NEW SCARECROW APPEARED

AND THE LONELY SCARECROW

FELT LESS ALONE

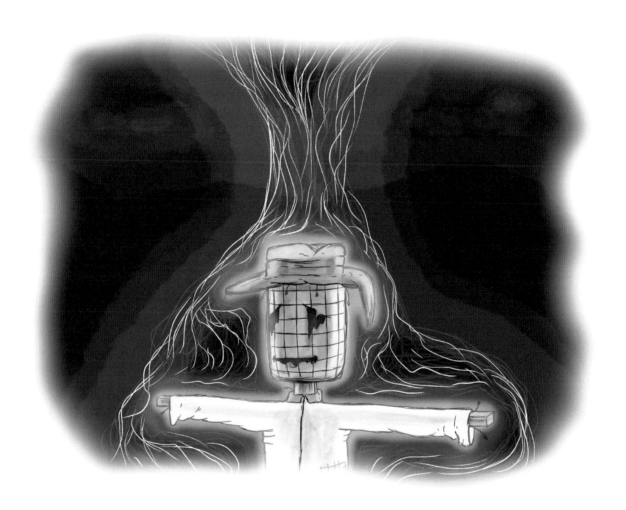

. . .

THIS GAVE HIM THE STRENGTH

TO STAND UP ON NEW LEGS

AND RUN TO THE DISTANT FIELD

EATING THE CROWS FOR POWER

UNTIL HE FOUND OUT

HIS NEW FRIEND

WAS JUST A WASHING LINE

. . .

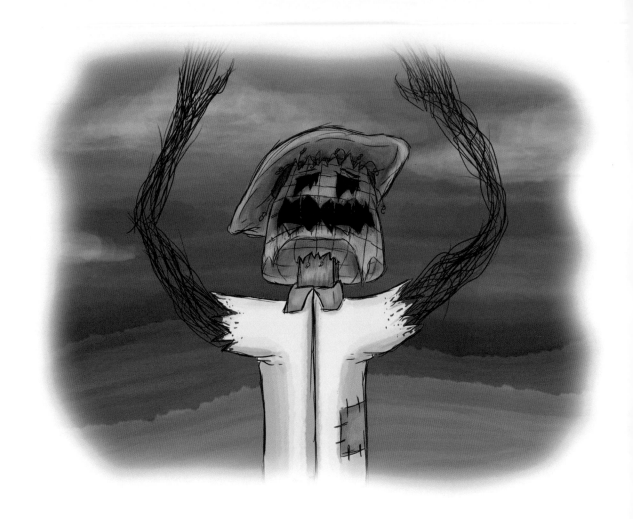

THE LONELINESS TOOK HOLD

HIS EXISTENCE BEGAN TO UNRAVEL

AND HE PAINFULLY FADED AWAY

THE END

Printed in Great Britain
by Amazon

24550258R00018